ISBN-13: 978-0-9976017-1-8

Published by: Witness Publishing Group, LLC

Ridgeland, South Carolina

www.witnesspublishing.com

Text copyright © 2016 by Joseph and Nickala Major

Illustrations © 2016 by Joseph and Nickala Major

All rights reserved. No part of this book may be reproduced in any written, electronic,

Recording, or photocopying without written permission of the publisher or author.

Printed and bound in the United States of America

Designed by Katherine Lindholm, Bizzy Bzzz Graphic Design and Witness Publishing Group, LLC

Editing by: Lenardo B. Youmans

Dedicated to our children– Khaliyah and James

Have you ever been hungry

and not had any food to eat?

Have you ever been

scared or afraid?

Have you ever been

sick or not felt well?

Have you ever been

picked on or made fun of?

Have you ever been

sad or felt hurt?

Love Him back

because that is all He wants from us!

what are some of
of the ways

in which you can show
your love for God?

God gave us the Ten Commandments to teach us how to love Him and love each other.

- Do not worship any other gods
- Do not make any idols
- Do not misuse God's name
- Keep the sabbath holy
- Honour your father & mother
- Do not murder
- Do not commit adultery
- Do not steal
- Do not lie
- Do not covet

Loving your neighbors, friends, strangers, and the poor by being nice to them and helping them out

is an awesome way to show God that you love Him.

The bible teaches that we are supposed to show respect for the authorities that God has allowed to be placed over us.

When we do this we are not only showing them respect, but we are also showing love and respect to God.

Police

Fire Department

Church

Those older than you

Teachers and Principals

The love of Jesus is real. After reading this book you should now know the different ways in which He shows us His love, and the ways in which you can show Him yours!

THE END

www.ingramcontent.com/pod-product-compliance
Lightning Source LLC
Chambersburg PA
CBHW041234040426
42444CB00002B/158